Piano/Vocal/Chords

80 YEARS OF POPULAR MUSIC

THE NINETIES

Project Manager: CAROL CUELLAR
Copy Editors: NADINE DEMARCO & DONNA SALZBURG
Cover Design: HEADLINE PUBLICITY LIMITED
Book Art Layout: LISA GREENE MANE

1990

Margaret Thatcher resigned from her office after 11 years as Prime Minister of England. Nelson Mandela was freed after 26 years in jail for his opposition to South Africa's white racist regime. Ivana Trump filed for divorce from her husband, Donald. It was the year for corn circles, bungee jumping, and New Kids on the Block, a five-piece singing group from Boston that became the nineties version of the Osmonds or The Jackson Five. On the way to a performance in Syracuse, New York, Gloria Estefan's tour bus crashed in Pennsylvania, leaving her with broken vertebrae.

1991

A 5,000-year-old man was discovered frozen deep in the Austrian Alps. Mines in the Persian Gulf during the Gulf War damaged the U.S. assault ship Tripoli and the guided missile cruiser Princeton. The Gulf War came to an end, a devastating defeat for Iraq. Martina Navratilova equaled Chris Evert's record of 157 career titles when she beat Monika Seles to win the Virginia Slims of California tournament in Oakland. Berenic Abbott, American photographer best known for her black-and-white studies of New York in the thirties, died at the age of 93.

1992

The new Euro Disney amusement park opened in Paris. Bill Clinton became President of the United States. Rioting occured in the streets of Southeast L.A. after four white police officers were acquitted of criminal wrongdoing despite videotape evidence.

1993

Federal agents raided the ranch where David Koresh, a religious cult leader, and 120 members were holed up. The siege ended in a terrible slaughter after officers opened fire and the building went up in flames. Seventeen children were among the dead. *Schindler's List*, a movie based on a true story of atrocities in Nazi Germany labor camps during the Holocaust, was a hit for producer Steven Spielberg. Strong opposition among several European members took place before approving the decision for Europe to become one, the European Union (EU). Great Britain was the last to ratify it.

1994

Nelson Mandela became President of South Africa. The U.N. approved U.S. soldiers' invasion of Haiti. Thirty people were killed when an earthquake hit the San Fernando Valley in California.

1995

O. J. Simpson was found not guilty of murdering his wife, Nicole Brown, and her friend, Ronald Goldman. The people of Oklahoma City, Oklahoma, and those across the nation were in a state of shock when terror hit their city: A bomb ripped apart the Alfred P. Murrah Federal Building, killing hundreds of men, women, and children.

1996

British beef was banned from several European countries after Mad Cow Disease, or BSE, was diagnosed. "Gangsta's Paradise," taken from the successful Michelle Pfieffer movie *Dangerous Minds*, was a hit for Coolio. It was a sad day for the people of England as Prince Charles and Lady Diana signed their divorce decree. A woman was killed and many were hurt when a bomb exploded in Centennial Park in Atlanta where the Olympic Games were being held.

1997

Hong Kong, a British colony since 1842, was passed back to China under an agreement signed in 1984. Princess Diana was laid to rest as thousands morned her tragic death and great loss to the nation. Elton John sang an adaptation of his hit "Candle in the Wind" at the funeral. That version became the biggest-selling single in history. Mother Teresa, a Roman Catholic nun known the world over for her work with the poor, died at the age of 87. The Spice Girls, an all-girl British group, hit the U.K. charts.

1998

Director James Cameron went into the record books with his blockbuster movie *Titanic*. Linda McCartney, wife of former Beatle Paul McCartney, lost her fight against cancer. Mark McGwire's 62nd home run of the season broke Roger Maris' 37-year-old record. Independent counsel Kenneth Starr sent a report to Congress accusing President Clinton of possible impeachable offenses. At the age of 77, John Glenn returned to orbit after 36 years. The federal government filed a sweeping anti-trust case against Microsoft Corp. America Online announced plans to buy Netscape in a $4.21 billion deal. The French Mint produced the first coins of Europe's single currency, the euro. Frank Sinatra died at the age of 82.

CONTENTS

YOUR LOVE AMAZES ME

Words and Music by
CHUCK JONES and AMANDA HUNT

Your Love Amazes Me - 4 - 1

5

Your Love Amazes Me - 4 - 2

Repeat ad lib. and fade

Verse 2:
I've seen a sunset that would make you cry,
And colors of a rainbow reaching 'cross the sky.
The moon in all its phases, but
Your love amazes me.
To Chorus:

Verse 3:
I've prayed for miracles that never came.
I got down on my knees in the pouring rain.
But only you could save me,
Your love amazes me.
(To Chorus:)

WHERE'S THE LOVE

Words and Music by
ISAAC HANSON, TAYLOR HANSON, ZACHARY HANSON,
MARK HUDSON and STEVEN SALOVER

Where's the Love - 6 - 1

Where's the Love - 6 - 4

ALL MY LIFE

Words and Music by
RORY BENNETT and
JO JO HAILEY

Chorus:

pray that___ you do love___ me too.___

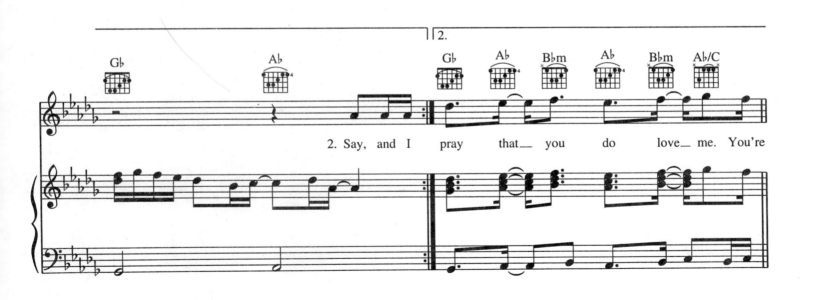

2. Say, and I pray that___ you do love___ me. You're

Bridge:

all that__ I ev - er know;__ when you smile__ on my face,__ all I see__ is a glow.__ You turn__

____ my life__ a - round,__ you pick__ me up____ when I____ was down.__ You're

all that I ev - er know; when you smile, my face glow. You pick me up when I was down. Say, you

all that I ev - er know; when you smile, my face glow. You pick me up when I was down. And I

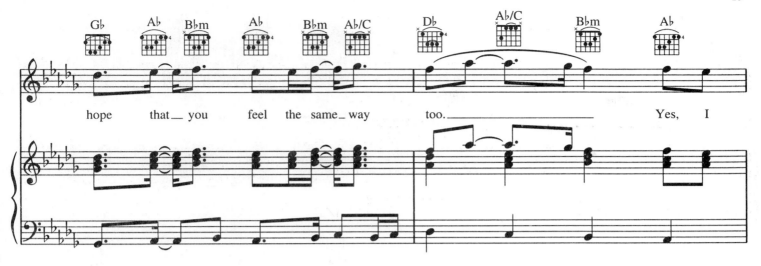

hope that ___ you feel the same ___ way too. _____ Yes, I

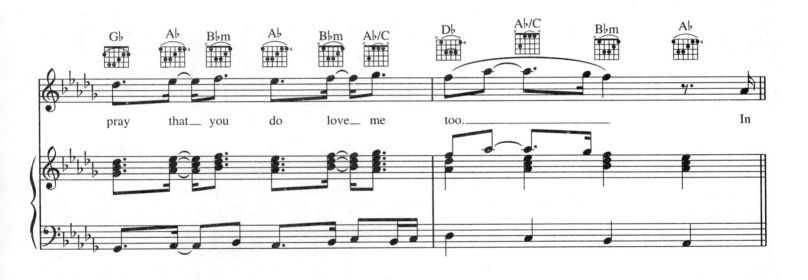

pray that ___ you do love ___ me too. _____ In

Chorus:

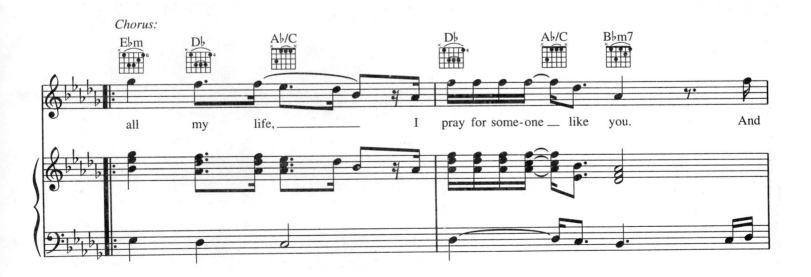

all my life, _____ I pray for some-one ___ like you. And

Verse 2:
Say, and I promise to never fall in love with a stranger.
You're all I'm thinkin', love, I praise the Lord above
For sendin' me your love, I cherish every hug.
I really love you so much.
(To Chorus:)

ANGEL EYES

Composed by
JIM BRICKMAN

Angel Eyes - 5 - 1

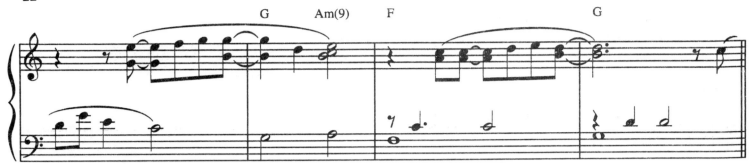

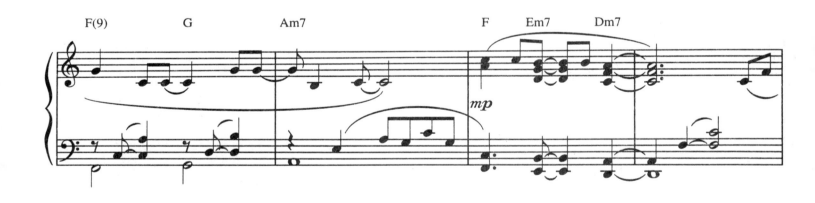

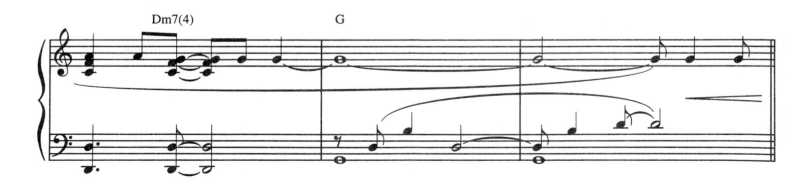

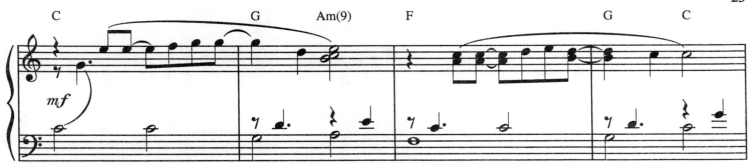

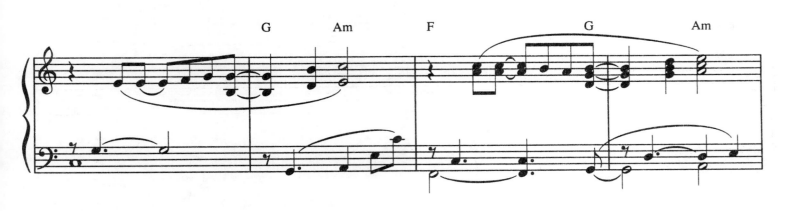

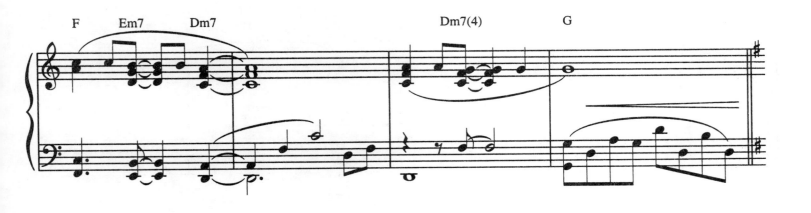

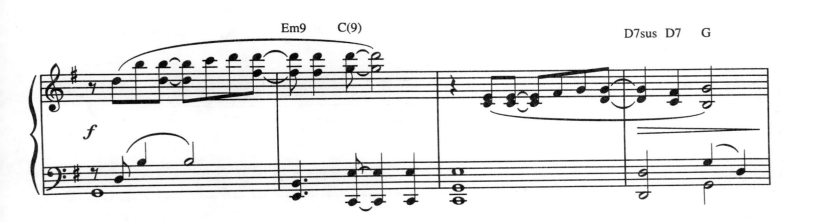

AS LONG AS YOU LOVE ME

By MAX MARTIN

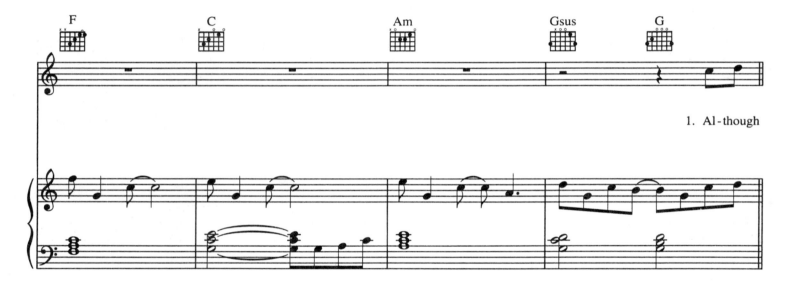

1. Al-though

lone - li - ness has al - ways been a friend of ___ mine, ___ I'm

As Long As You Love Me - 7 - 1

BECAUSE YOU LOVED ME
(Theme from "Up Close & Personal")

Words and Music by
DIANE WARREN

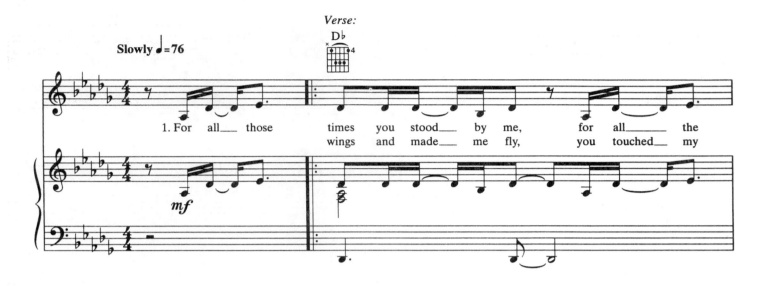

Because You Loved Me - 5 - 1

Because You Loved Me - 5 - 3

BREAKFAST AT TIFFANY'S

Words and Music by
TODD PIPES

Breakfast at Tiffany's - 5 - 1

39

Breakfast at Tiffany's - 5 - 2

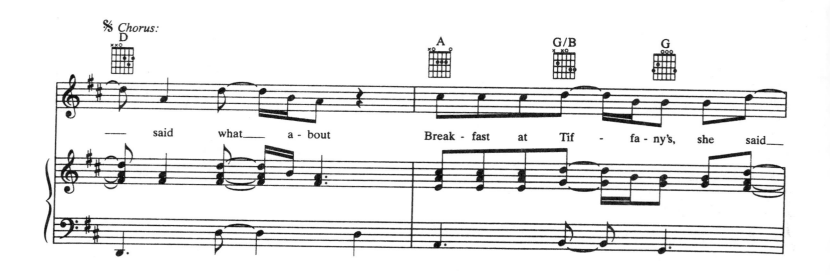

BUTTERFLY KISSES

Words and Music by
BOB CARLISLE and RANDY THOMAS

Butterfly Kisses - 7 - 1

46

Butterfly Kisses - 7 - 4

DREAMING OF YOU

Words and Music by
TOM SNOW and
FRANNE GOLDE

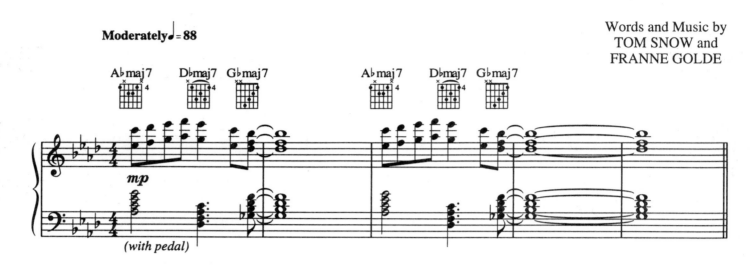

Verse:

1. Late at night when all the world___ is sleep-ing, I stay up and think of you.___ And I

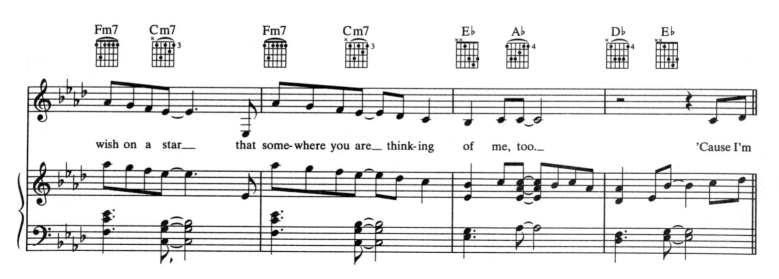

wish on a star___ that some-where you are___ think-ing of me, too.___ 'Cause I'm

Dreaming of You - 6 - 1

FOOLISH GAMES

Words and Music by
JEWEL KILCHER

* Vocal sung one octave lower

Foolish Games - 3 - 1

Verse 2:
You're always the mysterious one with
Dark eyes and careless hair,
You were fashionably sensitive
But too cool to care.
You stood in my doorway with nothing to say
Besides some comment on the weather.
(To Pre-Chorus:)

Verse 3:
You're always brilliant in the morning,
Smoking your cigarettes and talking over coffee.
Your philosophies on art, Baroque moved you.
You loved Mozart and you'd speak of your loved ones
As I clumsily strummed my guitar.

Verse 4:
You'd teach me of honest things,
Things that were daring, things that were clean.
Things that knew what an honest dollar did mean.
I hid my soiled hands behind my back.
Somewhere along the line, I must have gone
Off track with you.

Pre-Chorus 2:
Excuse me, think I've mistaken you for somebody else,
Somebody who gave a damn, somebody more like myself.
(To Chorus:)

FOR YOU I WILL

Words and Music by
DIANE WARREN

For You I Will - 5 - 1

(I Wanna Take) FOREVER TONIGHT

Words and Music by
ANDY GOLDMARK and ERIC CARMEN

Slowly ♩ = 92

1. Feel your breath_

Verse:

— on my shoul - der,   and I   know we could-n't get an - y clos -

— I'm on fi - re,   you're the   on - ly one I'll ev - er de - sire._

(I Wanna Take) Forever Tonight - 6 - 1

66 Chorus:

FOREVER'S AS FAR AS I'LL GO

Words and Music by
MIKE REID

Forever's As Far As I'll Go - 3 - 1

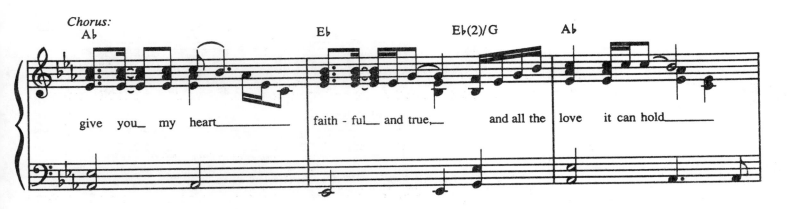

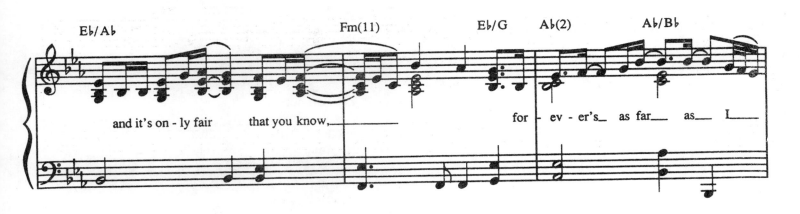

Forever's As Far As I'll Go - 3 - 2

Verse 2:
When there's age around my eyes and gray in your hair,
And it only takes a touch to recall the love we've shared.
I won't take for granted that you know my love is true.
Each night in your arms, I will whisper to you...
(To Chorus:)

FROM THIS MOMENT ON

Words and Music by
SHANIA TWAIN and R.J. LANGE

From This Moment On - 7 - 1

74

76

From This Moment On - 7 - 5

78

From This Moment On - 7 - 6

FROM A DISTANCE

Lyrics and Music by
JULIE GOLD

Slowly ♩ = 66

with Pedal

Verse:

1. From a dis-tance, the world looks blue and green, and the snow - capped moun - tains white. From a dis-tance, the o - cean meets the stream, and the ea - gle takes to

From a Distance - 4 - 1

Verse 2:
From a distance, we all have enough,
And no one is in need.
There are no guns, no bombs, no diseases,
No hungry mouths to feed.
From a distance, we are instruments
Marching in a common band;
Playing songs of hope, playing songs of peace,
They're the songs of every man.
(To Bridge:)

Verse 3:
From a distance, you look like my friend
Even though we are at war.
From a distance I just cannot comprehend
What all this fighting is for.
From a distance there is harmony
And it echos through the land.
It's the hope of hopes, it's the love of loves.
It's the heart of every man.

GOTHAM CITY

Words and Music by
R. KELLY

Verse:

1. Look-ing o - ver the sky-line of_____ the cit - y._____
2. Sleep-ing a - wake be - cause_____ of fear._____

Gotham City - 5 - 1

HANDS

Words and Music by
JEWEL KILCHER and PATRICK LEONARD

Moderately ♩ = 68

Tune guitar down a half step

1. If I could tell the world just one thing, it would be that we're all o - kay.
2. *See additional lyrics*

And not to wor - ry, 'cause wor - ry is waste - ful and use -

Hands - 5 - 1

less in times like these.___   I won't be made use-less.

I won't be i - dle with de - spair.   I will gath-er my-self a - round___

___ my faith,___ for light does the dark - ness most fear.

𝄋 *Chorus:*

My hands___ are small, I know.___ But they're not yours,___ they are___

Hands - 5 - 3

Repeat ad lib. and fade

Verse 2:
Poverty stole your golden shoes,
It didn't steal your laughter.
And heartache came to visit me,
But I knew it wasn't ever after.
We'll fight not out of spite,
For someone must stand up for what's right.
'Cause where there's a man who has no voice,
There ours shall go on singing.
(To Chorus:)

From the Original Motion Picture Soundtrack "DON JUAN DeMARCO"

HAVE YOU EVER REALLY LOVED A WOMAN?

Lyrics by
BRYAN ADAMS and ROBERT JOHN "MUTT" LANGE

Music by
MICHAEL KAMEN

Have You Ever Really Loved a Woman? - 6 - 1

last_____ for-ev - er.
be_____ to-geth - er. }

So tell me, have you ev-er real - ly, real-ly, real-ly, ev-er loved__ a

wom-an?_____

2. To real-ly love a wom-an._____ You've got to

Bridge:

give her some faith, hold her__ tight, a lit-tle ten-der - ness. You've got to treat her__ right!

From the Touchstone Motion Picture "CON AIR"

HOW DO I LIVE

Words and Music by
DIANE WARREN

How Do I Live - 4 - 1

now how do I, oh, how do I live

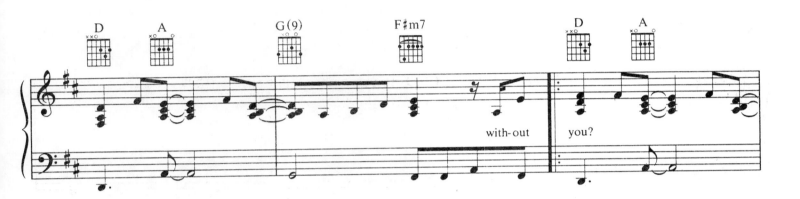

with-out you?

Repeat ad lib. and fade
(vocal 1st time only)

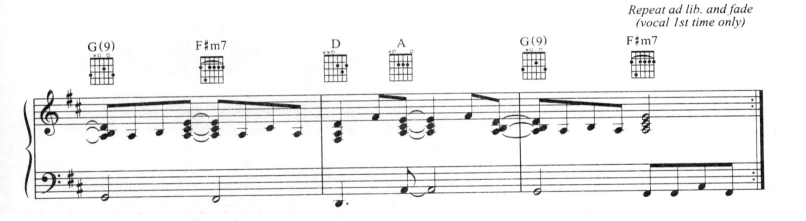

Verse 2:
Without you, there'd be no sun in my sky,
There would be no love in my life,
There'd be no world left for me.
And I, baby, I don't know what I would do,
I'd be lost if I lost you.
If you ever leave,
Baby, you would take away everything real in my life.
And tell me now...
(To Chorus:)

From the Original Soundtrack Album "THE PREACHER'S WIFE"

I BELIEVE IN YOU AND ME

Words and Music by
SANDY LINZER and DAVID WOLFERT

I Believe in You and Me - 4 - 1

Verse 2:
I will never leave your side,
I will never hurt your pride.
When all the chips are down,
I will always be around,
Just to be right where you are, my love.
Oh, I love you, boy.
I will never leave you out,
I will always let you in
To places no one has ever been.
Deep inside, can't you see?
I believe in you and me.
(To Bridge:)

I Believe in You and Me - 4 - 4

I BELIEVE I CAN FLY

Words and Music by
R. KELLY

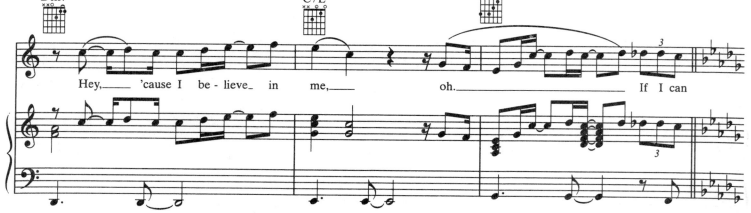

I Believe I Can Fly - 5 - 4

I Believe I Can Fly - 5 - 5

(EVERYTHING I DO) I DO IT FOR YOU

Lyrics and Music by
BRYAN ADAMS, R.J. LANGE and M. KAMEN

(Everything I Do) I Do It for You - 5 - 1

more____love. There's no - where____ un - less you're_ there, all the

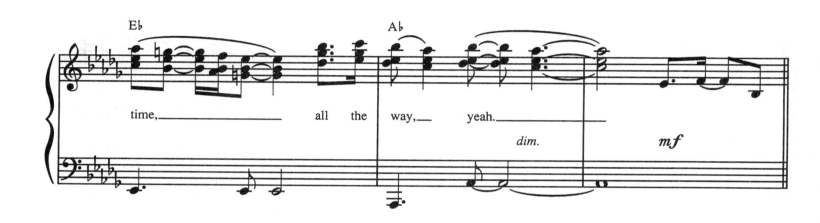

time,_____ all the way,___ yeah._____

dim.

mf

(instrumental solo . . .

Oh, you can't tell me it's not worth try - in'

. . . end solo)

From Touchstone Pictures' "ARMAGEDDON"

I DON'T WANT TO MISS A THING

Words and Music by
DIANE WARREN

I Don't Want to Miss a Thing - 7 - 1

I LOVE YOU ALWAYS FOREVER

Words and Music by
DONNA LEWIS

I Love You Always Forever - 5 - 1

"I LOVE YOU ALWAYS FOREVER" is inspired by the H.E. Bates Novel "LOVE FOR LYDIA."
Chorus/Bridge lyric courtesy of MICHAEL JOSEPH LTD. and THE ESTATE OF H.E. BATES.

126

2. Those days___ of warm rains come rush-ing back___ to me, miles of
3. *See additional lyrics*

wind - less,___ sum - mer night air. Se - cret

I Love You Always Forever - 5 - 2

I Love You Always Forever - 5 - 3

128

I Love You Always Forever - 5 - 4

129

Verse 3:
You've got the most unbelievable blue eyes I've ever seen.
You've got me almost melting away as we lay there
Under blue sky with pure white stars,
Exotic sweetness, a magical time.
(To Chorus:)

I Love You Always Forever - 5 - 5

From the Motion Picture "THE MIRROR HAS TWO FACES"

I FINALLY FOUND SOMEONE

Words and Music by
BARBRA STREISAND, MARVIN HAMLISCH,
R. J. LANGE and BRYAN ADAMS

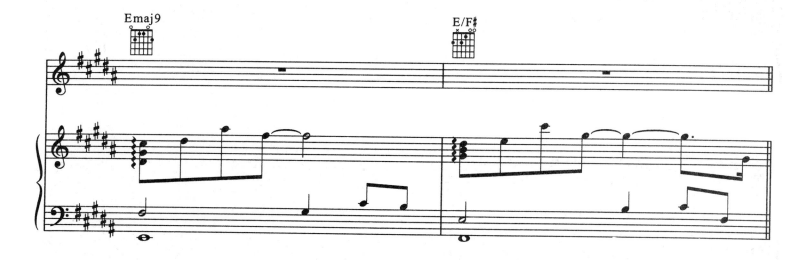

I Finally Found Someone - 8 - 1

132

I Finally Found Someone - 8 - 3

136

I SAY A LITTLE PRAYER

Words by
HAL DAVID

Music by
BURT BACHARACH

Chorus:

I SWEAR

Words and Music by
GARY BAKER and FRANK MYERS

Additional lyrics

2. I'll give you everything I can,
    I'll build your dreams with these two hands,
    And we'll hang some memories on the wall.
    And when there's silver in your hair,
    You won't have to ask if I still care,
    'Cause as time turns the page my love won't age at all.
    (To Chorus)

I WILL ALWAYS LOVE YOU

Words and Music by
DOLLY PARTON

I Will Always Love You - 5 - 1

Verse 3: Instrumental solo

Verse 4:
I hope life treats you kind
And I hope you have all you've dreamed of.
And I wish to you, joy and happiness.
But above all this, I wish you love.
(To Chorus:)

IN THIS LIFE

Words and Music by
MIKE REID and
ALLEN SHAMBLIN

154

In This Life - 3 - 2

Verse 2:
For every mountain I have climbed.
Every raging river crossed,
You were the treasure that I longed to find.
Without your love I would be lost.
(To Chorus:)

I WILL COME TO YOU

Words and Music by
ISAAC HANSON, TAYLOR HANSON,
ZACHARY HANSON, BARRY MANN and CYNTHIA WEIL

I Will Come to You - 6 - 2

158

160

I Will Come to You - 6 - 5

I'LL BE THERE FOR YOU
(Theme from "Friends")

Words by
DAVID CRANE, MARTA KAUFFMAN, ALLEE WILLIS,
PHIL SOLEM and DANNY WILDE

Music by
MICHAEL SKLOFF

I'll Be There for You - 6 - 1

164

* Guitar fill reads 8va.

I'll Be There for You - 6 - 3

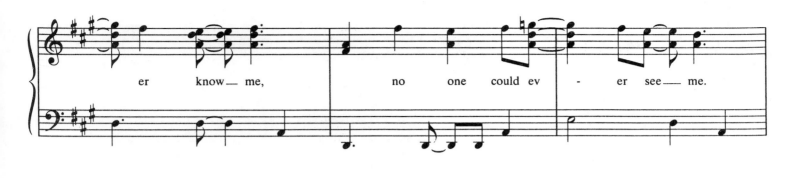

er know— me, no one could ev - er see— me.

Seems you're the on - ly one— who knows— what it's

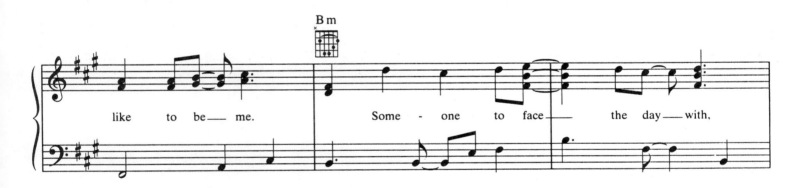

like to be— me. Some - one to face— the day— with,

make it through all— the rest— with, some - one I'll al -

166

I'll Be There for You - 6 - 5

167

I'll Be There for You - 6 - 6

I'M YOUR ANGEL

Words and Music by
R. KELLY

I'm Your Angel - 6 - 4

voic - es when you call___ me. I am your an - gel. And when all___

hope is gone,__ I'm here._ No mat - ter how far you are,__ I'm near._ It makes no__

dif - fer - ence who you are,__ I am your an - gel. I'll be your

Repeat ad lib. and fade

KISS FROM A ROSE

Words and Music by
SEAL

© 1994 PERFECT SONGS LIMITED, 42 - 46 St. Luke's Mews, London W11
All Rights Reserved

178

Kiss From a Rose - 6 - 5

me you're like a growing ad-dic-tion that I can't de-ny. Now, won't you tell me, is that

health-y ba-by? But did you know that when it snows, my eyes be-come large and the

D.%. al Coda   **⊕ CODA**

light that you shine can't be seen? Ba   da.   Now that your

rose is in bloom, a light hits the gloom__ on__ the__ bay.

KISSING YOU
(Love Theme from ''ROMEO + JULIET'')

Words and Music by
DES'REE and TIM ATACK

MMMBOP

Words and Music by
ISAAC HANSON, TAYLOR HANSON
and ZAC HANSON

Mmmbop - 7 - 1

186 *Verse:*

MISLED

Words and Music by
PETER ZIZZO and JIMMY BRALOWER

Misled - 5 - 1

Chorus:

194

Misled - 5 - 4

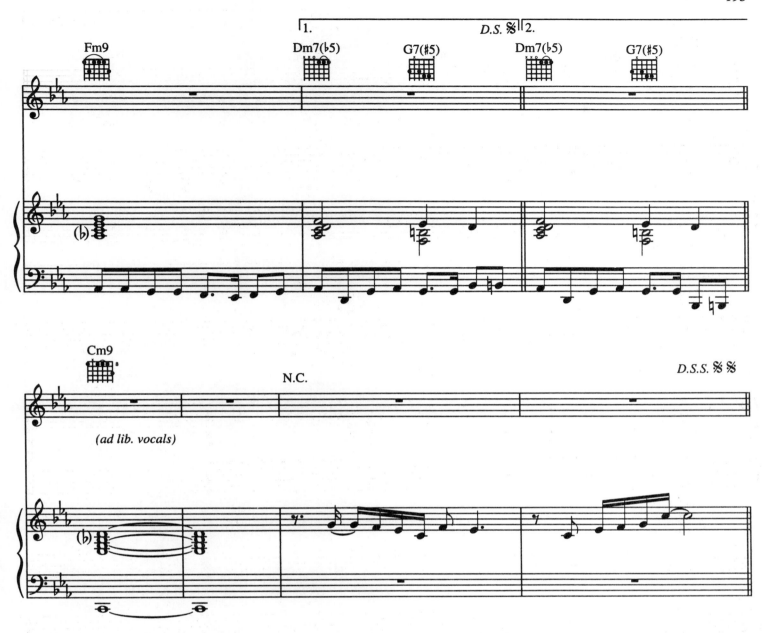

Verse 2:
Lovin' somebody ain't your average 9 to 5.
It takes conviction, it takes a will to survive.
I'm not somebody who commits the crime and leaves the scene.
But when I've been dissed, I don't spend much time on what might've been.

Bridges 2 & 3:
I'm not about self-pity, your love did me wrong,
So I'm movin', movin' on.
(To Chorus:)

MACARENA

Words and Music by
ANTONIO ROMERO and RAFAEL RUIZ

Coro:

Da - le a tu cuer - po a-le-grí - a Ma-ca-re-na que tu cuer-po es pa' dar - le a-le-grí-a y co-sa bue-na.

Macarena - 6 - 1

Macarena - 6 - 2

Da - le a tu cuer - po a - le - grí - a Ma - ca - re - na,   eh,_____ Ma - ca - re - na.

Verso 3:
Macarena sueña con el Corte inglés
Y se compra los modelos mas modernos.
Le gustaría vivir en Nueva York
Y ligar un novio nuevo.

Puente 2:
Macarena sueña con el Corte inglés
Y se compra los modelos mas modernos.
Le gustaría vivir en Nueva York
Y ligar un novio nuevo.
(Al Coro:)

Verso 4:
Macarena tiene un novio que se llama,
Que se llama de apellido Vitorino.
Y en la jura de bandera del muchacho
Se la dió con dos amigos.

Puente 3:
Macarena tiene un novio que se llama,
Que se llama de apellido Vitorino.
Y en la jura de bandera del muchacho
Se la dió con dos amigos.
(Al Coro:)

MORE THAN WORDS

Lyrics and Music by
BETTENCOURT, CHERONE

1. Say-in', "I__ love__ you" is not the words_ I want_

_ to__ hear_ from you.____ It's not that I____ want___ you not to say.__ But if_

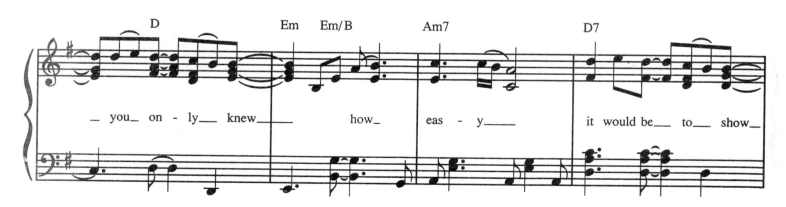

_ you_ on - ly__ knew____ how_ eas - y____ it would be___ to___ show_

More Than Words - 4 - 1

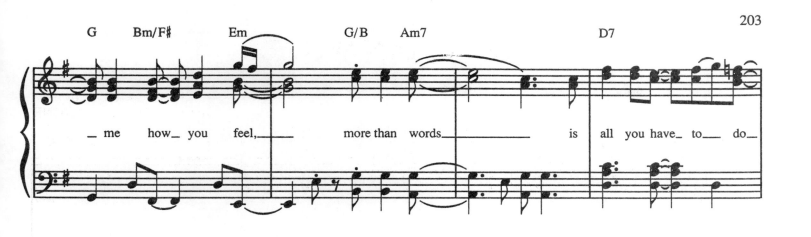

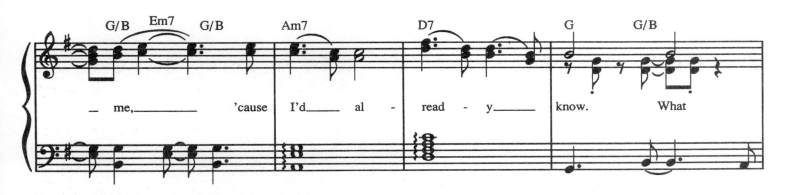

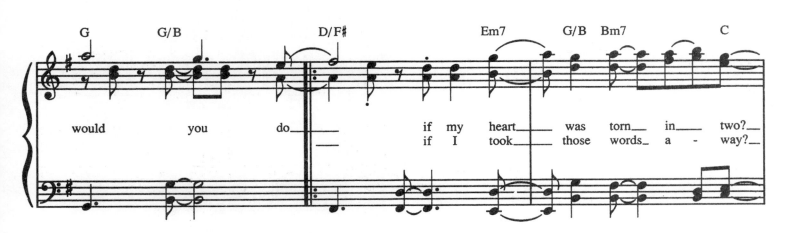

More Than Words - 4 - 2

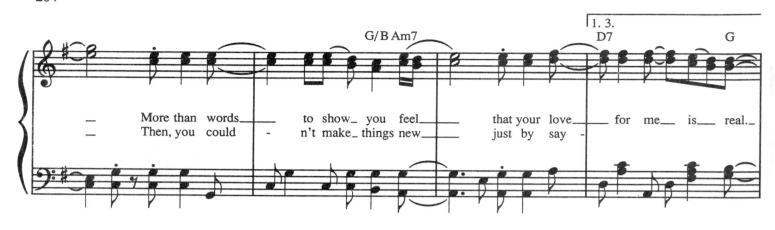

More Than Words - 4 - 3

Verse 2:
Now that I have tried to talk to you
And make you understand.
All you have to do is close your eyes
And just reach out your hands.
And touch me, hold me close, don't ever let me go.
More than words is all I ever needed you to show.
Then you wouldn't have to say
That you love me 'cause I'd already know.
(To Chorus:)

MY ONE TRUE FRIEND

(From "ONE TRUE THING")

Words and Music by
CAROLE BAYER SAGER, CAROLE KING
and DAVID FOSTER

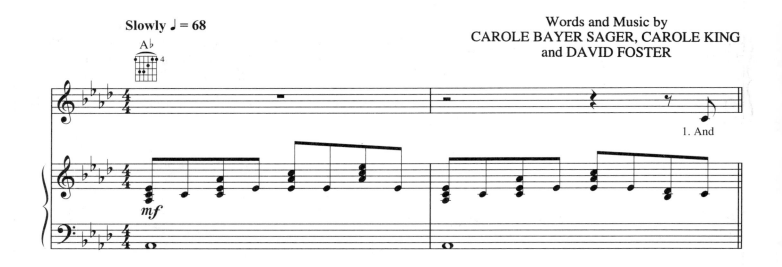

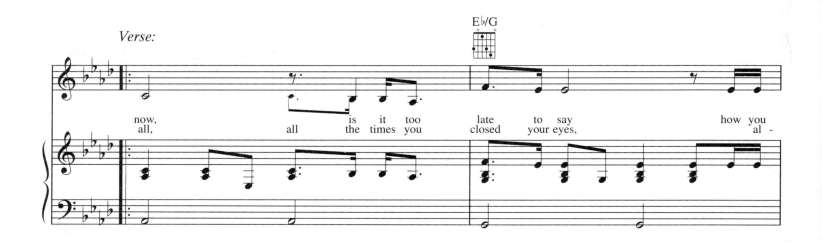

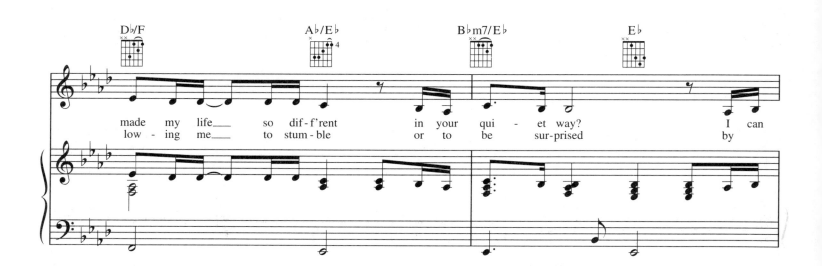

My One True Friend - 5 - 1

see_____ the joy____ in sim - ple things; a sun - lit
life_____ with all____ its twists and turns. I've made mis -

sky and all____ the songs____ we used to sing. I have
takes; you al - ways knew____ that I would learn. And when I

walked and I have prayed I could for -
left, it's you who stayed. You al - ways

give and we could start a - gain. In_____ the
knew that I'd come home a - gain. In_____ the

210

My One True Friend - 5 - 5

ONE OF US

Words and Music by
ERIC BAZILIAN

One of Us - 5 - 1

213

One of Us - 5 - 3

One of Us - 5 - 5

NOW AND FOREVER

Words and Music by
RICHARD MARX

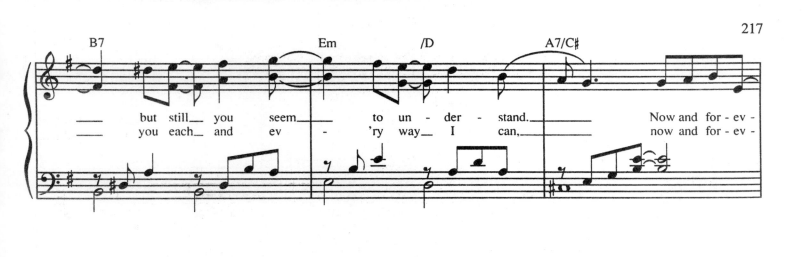

OH HOW THE YEARS GO BY

Words and Music by
WILL JENNINGS and SIMON CLIMIE

Oh How the Years Go By - 6 - 1

222

Oh How the Years Go By - 6 - 4

Verse 2:
There were times we stumbled,
They thought they had us down,
We came around.
How we rolled and rambled,
We got lost and we got found.
Now we're back on solid ground.
We took everything
All our times would bring
In this world of danger.
'Cause when your heart is strong,
You know you're not alone
In this world of strangers.
(To Chorus:)

QUIT PLAYING GAMES
(With My Heart)

Words and Music by
MAX MARTIN and HERBERT CRICHLOW

228

Verse 2:
I live my life the way,
To keep you comin' back to me.
Everything I do is for you,
So what is it that you can't see?
Sometimes I wish I could turn back time,
Impossible as it may seem.
But I wish I could so bad, baby
You better quit playing games with my heart.

SAY YOU'LL BE THERE

Words and Music by
SPICE GIRLS and
ELIOT KENNEDY

Say You'll Be There - 5 - 1

234

Say You'll Be There - 5 - 4

Verse 2:
If you put two and two together you will see what our friendship is for,
If you can't work this equation then I guess I'll have to show you the door,
There is no need to say you love me it would be better left unsaid.

I'm giving you everything all that joy can bring this I swear,
And all that I want from you is a promise you will be there,
Yeah I want you.

Verse 3: (Instrumental)
Any fool can see they're falling, gotta make you understand.
To Coda

From the Lucasfilm Ltd. Productions ''STAR WARS'', ''THE EMPIRE STRIKES BACK''
and ''RETURN OF THE JEDI'' - Twentieth Century-Fox Releases.

STAR WARS
(Main Theme)

Music by
JOHN WILLIAMS

Star Wars - 2 - 1

SUNNY CAME HOME

Words and Music by
SHAWN COLVIN and JOHN LEVENTHAL

Sunny Came Home - 6 - 1

240

242

TEARS IN HEAVEN

Moderately slow ♩ = 80

Words and Music by
WILL JENNINGS and ERIC CLAPTON

(with pedal)

Verse:

1. Would you know my name _____ if I saw you in heav-
2. Would you hold my hand _____ if I saw you in heav-

en?
en? Would it be the same _____
Would you help me stand _____

if I saw you in heav - en?
if I saw you in heav - en? I must be strong_____
I'll find my way_____

Tears in Heaven - 4 - 1

TELL HIM

Words and Music by
LINDA THOMPSON, DAVID FOSTER
and WALTER AFANASIEFF

Tell Him - 6 - 1

252

Tell Him - 6 - 5

Verse 2:
(Barbra:)
Touch him with the gentleness you feel inside. (*C:* I feel it.)
Your love can't be denied.
The truth will set you free.
You'll have what's meant to be.
All in time, you'll see.
(Celine:)
I love him, *(B: Then show him.)*
Of that much I can be sure. *(B: Hold him close to you.)*
I don't think I could endure
If I let him walk away
When I have so much to say.
(To Chorus:)

From the Twentieth Century Fox Motion Picture

THAT THING YOU DO!

Words and Music by
ADAM SCHLESINGER

THINK TWICE

Words and Music by
ANDY HILL and PETE SINFIELD

Think Twice - 3 - 1

Think Twice - 3 - 2

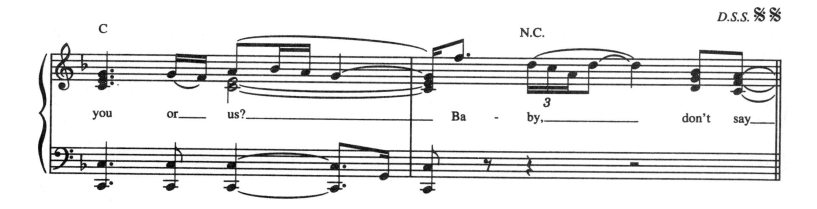

Verse 2:
Baby, think twice for the sake of our love, for the memory,
For the fire and the faith that was you and me.
Baby, I know it ain't easy when your soul cries out for higher ground,
'Cos when you're halfway up, you're always halfway down.
But baby, this is serious.
Are you thinking 'bout you or us?
(To Chorus:)

Chorus 4:
Don't do what you're about to do.
My everything depends on you,
And whatever it takes, I'll sacrifice.
Before you roll those dice,
Baby, think twice.

TIME TO SAY GOODBYE
(Con Te Partiró)

Lyrics by LUCIO QUARANTOTTO
English Lyrics by FRANK PETERSON

Music by
FRANCESCO SARTORI

Slowly ♩ = 60

Verse 1:

1. Quan - do so - no so - lo so - gno_al-l'o - riz - zon-te_e man - can le pa -

ro - le, sì lo so che non c'è lu-ce_in u - na stan - za quan-do man-ca_il

Time to Say Goodbye - 5 - 1

264

Time to Say Goodbye - 5 - 4

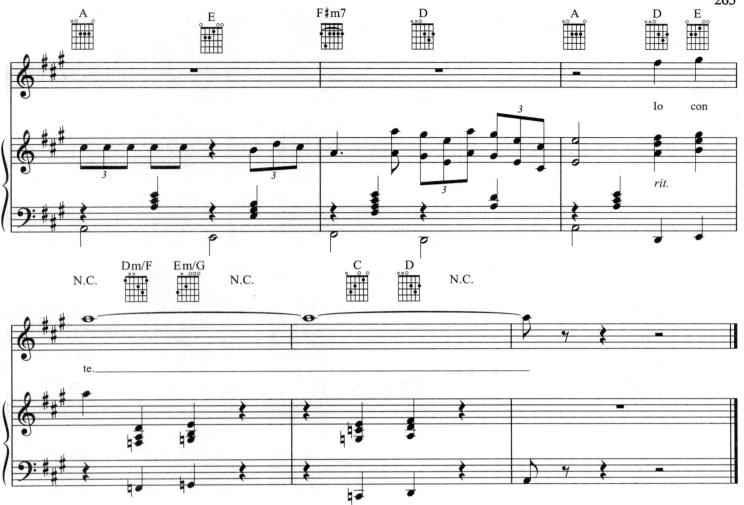

English literal translation:
Verse 1:
When I'm alone,
I dream of the horizon
And words fail me.
There is no light
In a room where there is no sun.
And there is no sun if you're not here
With me, with me.
From every window,
Unfurl my heart,
The heart that you have won.
Into me you've poured the light,
The light that you've found
By the side of the road.

Chorus:
Time to say goodbye.
Places that I've never seen
Or experienced with you,
Now I shall.
I'll sail with you upon ships across the seas,
Seas that exist no more.
It's time to say goodbye.

Verse 2:
When you're far away,
I dream of the horizon
And words fail me.
And of course, I know that you're with me,
With me.
You, my moon, you are with me.
My sun, you're here with me,
With me, with me, with me.

Chorus:
Time to say goodbye.
Places that I've never seen
Or experienced with you,
Now I shall.
I'll sail with you upon ships across the seas,
Seas that exist no more,
I'll revive them with you.

Tag:
I'll go with you upon ships across the seas,
Seas that exist no more,
I'll revive them with you.
I'll go with you,
I'll go with you.

TOO LATE, TOO SOON

Words and Music by
JON SECADA, JAMES HARRIS III
and TERRY LEWIS

Too Late, Too Soon - 4 - 1

Verse 2:
I wish I would have known,
I wouldn't have left you all alone.
Temptation led you wrong.
Tell me how long this has been goin' on?
'Cause I thought our love was strong,
But I guess I must be dreamin'.
(To Chorus:)

YOU WERE MEANT FOR ME

Words and Music by
JEWEL KILCHER and STEVE POLTZ

273

You Were Meant for Me - 5 - 4

Coda

I was meant for you. Yeah,___ you were

meant for me and I was meant for you.___

Verse 2:
I called my mama, she was out for a walk.
Consoled a cup of coffee, but it didn't wanna talk.
So I picked up a paper, it was more bad news,
More hearts being broken or people being used.
Put on my coat in the pouring rain.
I saw a movie, it just wasn't the same,
'Cause it was happy and I was sad,
And it made me miss you, oh, so bad.
(To Chorus:)

Verse 3:
I brush my teeth and put the cap back on,
I know you hate it when I leave the light on.
I pick a book up and then I turn the sheets down,
And then I take a breath and a good look around.
Put on my pj's and hop into bed.
I'm half alive but I feel mostly dead.
I try and tell myself it'll be all right,
I just shouldn't think anymore tonight.
(To Chorus:)

UN-BREAK MY HEART

Words and Music by
DIANE WARREN

Un-Break My Heart - 5 - 1

278

Un-Break My Heart - 5 - 4

VALENTINE

Composed by
JIM BRICKMAN and
JACK KUGELL

Moderately ♩ = 92

(with pedal)

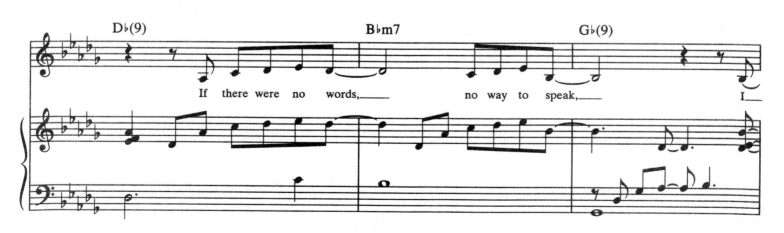

If there were no words,___ no way to speak,___ I

Valentine - 6 - 1

282

Valentine - 6 - 3

284

Valentine - 6 - 5

WALKIN' ON THE SUN

Words and Music by
STEVE HARWELL, GREGORY CAMP,
PAUL DeLISLE and KEVIN COLEMAN

Walkin' on the Sun - 6 - 1

world to snuff_ the fi - res and the li - ars. Hey, I know it's just a song, but it's spice_

_ for the rec - i - pe. This is a love at - tack,_ I know it went out, but it's back._ It's just like

an - y fad,_ it re - tracts_ be - fore im - pact. And just like fash - ion, it's a pas - sion for the

with it and hip._ If you got the goods, they'll come and buy it just to stay in the clique._

288

Verse 2:
Twenty-five years ago they spoke out
And they broke out of recession and oppression.
And together they toked and they folked out with guitars
Around a bonfire, just singin' and clappin'; man, what the hell happened?
Yeah, some were spellbound, some were hell bound,
Some, they fell down and some got back up and fought back against the meltdown.
And their kids were hippie chicks, all hypocrites
Because their fashion is smashin' the true meaning of it.
(To Chorus:)

ALL I WANNA DO

Words and Music by
SHERYL CROW, WYN COOPER, KEVIN GILBERT,
BILL BOTTRELL and DAVID BAERWALD

294

All I Wanna Do - 8 - 3

Verse 3:
I like a good beer buzz early in the morning,
And Billy likes to peel the labels from his bottles of Bud
And shred them on the bar.
Then he lights every match in an oversized pack,
Letting each one burn down to his thick fingers
Before blowing and cursing them out.
And he's watching the Buds as they spin on the floor.
A happy couple enters the bar dancing dangerously close to one another.
The bartender looks up from his want ads.
(To Chorus:)

YOU'RE STILL THE ONE

Words and Music by
SHANIA TWAIN and R.J. LANGE

Verse 2:
Ain't nothin' better,
We beat the odds together.
I'm glad we didn't listen.
Look at what we would be missin'.
(To Bridge:)

The Best Personality Folios of 1998

JIM BRICKMAN—
Visions of Love
(PF9818) Piano Solos

GARTH BROOKS—
The Limited Series
(PF9823) Piano/Vocal/Chords

DAYS OF THE NEW—
Days of the New
(0230B) Authentic GUITAR-TAB Edition

CELINE DION—
Let's Talk About Love
(PF9813) Piano/Vocal/Chords

DREAM THEATER—
Falling into Infinity
(0209B) Authentic GUITAR-TAB Edition

FLEETWOOD MAC—
The Dance
(PF9742) Piano/Vocal/Chords

FLEETWOOD MAC—
Guitar Anthology Series
(PG9717) Authentic GUITAR-TAB Edition

GREEN DAY—
Nimrod
(0224C) Authentic GUITAR-TAB Edition

JEWEL—
Spirit
(PF9836) Piano/Vocal/Chords
(PG9810) Guitar/Vocal with Tablature

KORN—
Follow the Leader
(0308B) Authentic GUITAR-TAB Edition

MADONNA—
Ray of Light
(0263B) Piano/Vocal/Chords

JIMMY PAGE & ROBERT PLANT—
Walking into Clarksdale
(6385A) Guitar/Tab/Vocal

PANTERA—
Guitar Anthology Series
(0223B) Authentic GUITAR-TAB Edition

LEANN RIMES—
You Light Up My Life:
Inspirational Songs
(PF9737) Piano/Vocal/Chords

SEMISONIC—
Feeling Strangely Fine
(0284B) Authentic GUITAR-TAB Edition

SMASHING PUMPKINS—
Adore
(PG9802) Authentic GUITAR-TAB Edition

SHANIA TWAIN—
Come On Over
(PF9746) Piano/Vocal/Chords

VAN HALEN—3
(0258B) Authentic GUITAR-TAB Edition

AD 0137

BIGGEST
POP HITS & COUNTRY HITS OF 1998

BIGGEST POP HITS OF 1998

(MF9820) Piano/Vocal/Chords
(AF9835) Easy Piano arr. Coates & Brimhall

- The biggest songs from the hottest artists
- More than 30 hit songs
- Available in P/V/C and Easy Piano Editions

Titles (and artists) include: **I Don't Want to Miss a Thing** (Aerosmith) • **My Heart Will Go On** (Celine Dion) • **How Do I Live** (LeAnn Rimes) • **You're Still the One** (Shania Twain) • **Ray of Light** (Madonna) • **All My Life** (K-Ci & Jo Jo) • **Good Riddance (Time of Your Life)** (Green Day) • **This Kiss** (Faith Hill) • **Kiss the Rain** (Billie Myers) • **Walkin' on the Sun** (Smash Mouth) and many more.

BIGGEST COUNTRY HITS OF 1998

(MF9819) Piano/Vocal/Chords

- The top country songs of the year
- The hottest country artists
- All of your favorites collected together in one great folio

Titles (and artists) include: **You're Still the One** (Shania Twain) • **This Kiss** (Faith Hill) • **Nothin' But the Taillights** (Clint Black) • **There's Your Trouble** (Dixie Chicks) • **How Do I Live** (LeAnn Rimes) • **From This Moment On** (Shania Twain & Bryan White) • **I Do (Cherish You)** (Mark Wills) • **Cover You in Kisses** (John Michael Montgomery) • **Bad Day to Let You Go** (Bryan White) • **Holes in the Floor of Heaven** (Steve Wariner) and many more.

AD 0138